AROUND THE FIRE

Poems by
Emiliano Martín

AROUND THE

FIRE

Poems by Emiliano Martín

Collection of original poems
based on life's observations, personal experience and a
scent of philosophical reflections added by the author.

ISBN # 978-1-71668-910-9

Printed in the U.S.A.
First Edition 2020
Lulu. Com

Emiliano Martín
Bensalem, PA., 19020
Poeta48@aol.com

To

all who

with honesty

believe in friendship

and worldwide peace...!

- INDEX -

ALL AROUND

Lyrics defining good music are easy to sing along
and that is what makes a good song.

So do not waste any time
looking for words without rhyme.

You see
the poem needs its own sound
with nice verses all around...

and you could help to write something
instead of thinking of nothing

while chances are passing by
disappearing in the sky

one round after another.

ANYTHING CAN BE BOUGHT

I always
told him about it.

The three most important things
we all need
when in the street
are:

money
a watch
and the keys.

Of course
with the keys
we could open any locked door.

The watch
will tell us when it
will be the time to do so.

And while having money
anything can be bought:

the watch
the keys
even the door.

That is not hard to believe...!

BEING IN PLACE

Scratching the surface
of any good deed
brings the opportunity
of obtaining peace
even a moment of grace
when all the logistics
are well put in place.

\- - -

FORMER FRIENDSHIP

When friendship has failed
and we can no longer maintain silence
about it...
there was no friendship nor did exist
a handy degree
of trust.

AROUND THE FIRE

People dance around the fire
yet no one shows the desire
to cut the cheese
or the bread.

Meanwhile the music's playing
louder than one could explain.

So the meal has to wait
while we would like to eat something
before the party may end.

Observing all that excitement
I remain everyone's friend
around an exciting fire
warming up with lively flames.

By now this may sound it is funny
but often I do maintain
an empty stomach
and no fuel in my head.

Feeling tired... even hungry
and ready to leave that place
I take steps... moving forward
since I always hate to wait.

EVENING'S GOOD BYE

Saying good bye to the evening
the sun sneaks out somehow
leaving us wondering if
the moon
will simply do
enough to shining on her own.

Saying good bye to the evening
where somehow there is no moon
there is a lament escaping
from each and every heart
crying out loud
for ideas
in search of hidden stars.

PERFECT

It was a confined space
hidden
away from the crowd.

Quiet
all around
no one could hear a sound.

Once inside
with no objects of distraction
a dim light shone for companion
and it was enough.

It became the perfect room
to find the truth.

FOR REFERENCE

Looking back
there is no future.

From the present
looking up straight ahead
we all find a question mark.

That must be an
earmark for reference
in the unknown days to come.

\- - -

BRANCHES AND LEAVES

When the branches of a tree
are no longer providing leaves...
it is over.

CHANGE OF PLANS

Once the journey was set
and we thought
to be willing
and ready to go.

The trip was long
the steps too short
but the energy required
was not to be found
till the time it was decided
to move back
and change the direction
of the original plan.

POSSIBILITY

Intimacy
in the open
holds no longer weight
for privacy.

That is why there is a possibility
to find one of the best poems ever written
and that has never been read...
residing among pages of a manuscript
own by its author and kept to himself.

PERSONAL GAIN

Often
there are no boundaries
for telling a lie
nor there is an attitude
to stop it
from spreading out
in the open fields of
personal gain.

Yet
for some
an agonizing pain is felt
while showing off thresholds of truth
that few
are able to see or hear... and others
don't care about.

That could
even damage or endure
the fiber made from
an alleged
decent behavior.

APPROACH TO WRITING A POEM

People write poetry for many reasons.
Induced by moody behavior
are the highlights
and low points of the day.

Preoccupations and ambition,
hate and love's exaltation,
disappointments, celebrations....
Any meaningful thought of importance
must be penned down,
shared among our peers. Making it happen.

We are privileged of having the gift of writing,
as much as our mood and inspiration allows us...
for fun, money, or simply pass the time.

We even write to show off
or just to the delightful experience
of discovering a universe waiting for the proper ink
over a blank piece of paper.

And there are ways to go about it easily,
without signals of indifference.

Like it happens on a date,
while writing we must be ready
and willing to create a good impression,
look for intimacy, show self assurance
and respect for the subject,

find the way to be convincing,
sincerely meaning
and conveying all that we need to say.

Grooming and style can be helpful.

Instead of a worn down pencil,
use a gorgeous fountain pen,
grasp the moment, make it yours,
and write on a clean piece of paper.

The result could be surprising...
with knowledge, talent and good luck.

WINGING IT OUT

On the wings of waiting
some of us remain at ease
at the sideline of no hope
lacking self esteem
at all...
others get caught up with errands
unable to become free.

Yet
when things are said and done
all that is left
falls
behind
memories...
often of the best kind
along deeds materialized
for the convenience of eyes
putting the good word for us.

UNNECESSARILY

Conflict is part of life
and inevitably so
it happens most of the time.

However
good intentions will define
the venues that we could follow
so that everything is finc.

Yet by adding
unnecessary excitement
we could easily clog the mind.
not to mention the reaction
from someone who is unkind.

CALM WITHIN THE STORM

A poem is not a poem
without using the right words
words captivating the senses
senses favoring the thought
any author calls his own.

A poem is a view point
crafted by feelings
style...
a way to deliver thinking
like no one else could provide.

Yes. A poem is a vision
reflections
the glimpse of deep appreciation
causing our admiration
for the style of written thoughts
seeking proper human voices
to proudly read words out loud.

A poem in written form
or recited to the world...
could well be joy
and true sadness.

It is calm within the storm.

SEEKING FREEDOM

When the sound comes from the river
the water never looks back
nor does it show signs of fear.

It maintains its own speed
seeking a chance to be free.

Yet facing a waterfall
the stream has no way to go
but down...

And within that sudden plunge
surges a mist in the air
to remind us of a song
that tragically went wrong.

TIME & EXPERIENCE

There is no need to worry
nor to fear any task
placed in front of our hands.

No reason to put aside
an idea... or to delay
a performance
forcing us to being late.

It is not wrong taking chances.
it is fine to exhibit courage
to welcome a risk
and try it out
once or twice.

Even if failure makes
one more attempt
to display
its ugly face
we must take the right steps
in a positive direction.

In simple terms... only time
and experience can improve
whatever we dare to do.

NOT FAIR

Poems come in many forms
lengths and subjects
yet they hold
issues in common
like verbal artifice
sounds in harmony with significance
and weight
through a meaningful narration
staying away from prose.

Surely there is good prose
bordering the scent of poetry
yet
masquerading it in verse
could result in a plain farce.

It is not fair to the poet
who is figuring out a reason
why to spend the time and vision
to convey a written thought
while looking for
a rhyming substance
rather than phrases of prose.

COLD AND HOT

I can be cold as an iceberg
yet I can also be hot
like an iron in the fire.
or the extremely steaming bath.

But it is not my desire
to circumvent an idea
by putting on an attire
just to make me go nuts
after being called a liar
when you tried to set me up.

By this time I had enough...!

SWEAT AND EFFORT

Never mind the road
we've taken
nor is it the finish line.

Feel proud of the sweat and effort
put in the steps left behind
with ambition and big heart.

BROODING VERSES

Looking here and there
I could not find anywhere
the things
I was looking for.

I did not give up
yet I feel
deep in my heart
the search must go on
to finish the song
I'm willing to impart ---
within sounds of brooding verses
few souls would consider art.

GREAT EXAMPLE

In life
it's not about being human.

It is behaving as such
with a demeanor
examples
actions
driven
by the heart.

The rest is just "oratory"
looking for ways to depart
from personal viewpoints of this
or that.

NO DISCOURAGEMENT

No discouragement is granted
to whom chooses moving up
within layers of adversity
where there is no way to advance.

And often... that is a fact.

This is why it is important
not to listen to anyone
especially while you are acting
solely in your own behalf.

Follow your instinct
till you feel just had enough
and perhaps you will realize
that your merit will surprise
the rest of us..

BITTERNESS

The pen was held in his fingers
while multiples sheets of white paper
patiently waited for words
to be easily disclosed.

Ready and willing
to pen down his thoughts
the poet kept trying
while thinking
sadly unaware of
a dysfunctional ink cartridge
making it hard to perform.

Some scratches on the paper
were left on display
simply 'cause the ink was dry
and there was no way to write
anymore.

Only bitterness escaped
out of the poet's voice.

END OF THE MEETING

Late evening
and looking for a chance
to catch up
they found the opportunity
to go through it
and end the meeting.

His arm was extended
to reach out for her hand.

Apparently guessing that move
was not clear to be followed up.

So there was silence
and quiet. Only one step back
took place without a shake of hands.

No words were spoken in such interact.
only disappointing glances...
were left behind
for the two moving shadows
losing their shape in the dark.

BEING STILL

Someone thought
that I was lazy
simply
'cause I was relaxing
on top of my own beliefs.

Please don't confuse
being still
with doing nothing at all.

For the power of imagination
could build wonders
while we dream on.

Even though we may still wake up
caught between layers of cold
there is hope
with the intervention
of a few good rhyming words.

ANCESTRY

With curiosity
and a degree of indulging reverence
I keep looking at the old photographs
my mother was so fond of.

They are still kept in a wooden box
yet some photos appeared to be damaged
by wrinkles and scratches produced by time.

My mother was very careful
she could only open that box
however she sat and share with all of us
the images of her ancestors.

I remember when she mentioned who
was who while running her finger
over the face of her folks.

They all had the serious look
nicely dressed up in Sunday clothes
the women standing up
right behind a seated man
there was much pride in their eyes.

I can see familiar faces
with recognizable features
making me shiver
but some names I can't remember

and my children do not care
even though I own that box.

\- - -

TANKA (Focusing)

The moving target
prevent me from focusing
when aiming at it.
That is why I take my time
waiting for a giant blast.

TREES

Nothing changes like a tree.

In the summer days
often majestic with branches and leafs
can provide shelter -
a total relief
for anyone looking for a nice shade
away from the heat.

And yet in the winter
appearing bare in the cold
while hit by the wind...
unconsciously driven by nature's will
the tree won't surrender
and manage to lead
the way to recovery.

A very slow process
expecting the Spring.

IN FOR A SURPRISE

Nature is not always fair
but it is what
we all have
and not at our command.

With dramatic consequences
when behaving in full force
it's prudent to run for cover
while patiently let it go.

Nature must follow its course
and if we add opposition
we are in for a surprise
'cause no one could fool around the
power contained within...
centuries of a behavior
that humans cannot believe.

Even with that sense of arrogance
and splendor on display
nature makes us hard to resist
to its temper or charming ways
to proceed.

IN WRITING

It happens to most of us
poets.

When pushed
by the muse...
almost in a ceremonial way
we figure out what to say
in writing.

Even though we spread out ink
over the surface of paper
some awareness
to reach greatness
or at least a deep concern
to write well
must
      be
         present
                  in the mind.

Otherwise we just pretend to be hiding
behind verses arousing the limit
of our own discontent
or happiness for that matter
since our human mood changes
         viciously
                  and often daily.

MY WORLD... YOUR WORLD

Huge and small
just like it can be hot
and cold
as amazing as simple
it remains out of reach
and yet so close.

We live in it
making us believe that it is ours.

We breathe in it
while assuming we posses it
but that is far from the truth
for our world simply own us
by allowing us to borrow
time...
while in it.

NO BLUFFER

Two months ago
the river was quiet
inviting us all
to enjoy its scenery.

Flowing at ease and smiling
with gentle waves in its current
it kept the nearby lands... dry.

Today things have changed
leaving us in disbelief.

The rain keeps on pouring
no one can stop it.

The river runs free
water picks up speed
and the current is wild
always looking for low ground
and damaging all around
or fertilizing at will
after all
the agonizing drought we've suffered
by now seems to be forgotten
yet the river is no bluffer.

SADDLE BAGS

Words of wisdom
can definitely be wisdom
but only coming from
well known
dead people
or perhaps those who are alive
riding the mule of success
with deep saddle bags of gold.

EXISTENCE ON EARTH

It is not how long we were
in this existence on Earth
but the many friends we made
and the footprints left behind
our temporary life
of circumstances
and sorrows
and joys
making a difference
in all of us
on how
we shall be remembered.

TWO PAINTERS

Two painters of universal appeal.
Yet, the question about them
seems to be always the same.

Who was better, Dalí or Picasso?

Well, they are two different styles
in color, flavor and taste,
in substance and provocative intentions.
for anything that they chased.

Although Cubism and Surrealism
could be an interchangeable asset
between both of them,
there is a unique seal of craftsmanship
applicable to each painter.

They were two giants from the same country
two pulsating hearts of greatness,
exuberant, brilliant minds showing off,
not just with their personality
but the merit of their work.

Of course, Dalí came later
wanting to learn from Picasso,
but by the end... with ambition of their own,
they both walked the sands of success,
crossed the finish line of redemption

with notoriety and wealth,
even self inflicted pain
underlined by circumstances
of some immoral strength
-- with a significant length
driven in separates ways.

\- - -

TANKA (Surprises)

People sharing thoughts
staggering words coming out
looking for answers
yet on the way to be heard
there are surprises.

MELTING

Time melting away hours
squashed by our deeds.

Days
unconsciously running
into weeks.

Months becoming years
while in retrospective
the next thing we know
seemingly appears that time
our time
is long gone
and out of site.

The facts will remain a memory
perhaps a photography
kept in an album
reminding us who we were
what it was...
and how it happened.

Somehow we keep waking up daily
looking for a horizon
with that special new morning
born in the melting of our life.

NO EXPLANATION

A dream will seek out a vision
and a vision needs a plan
but the plan without an effort
will collapse in no much time.

So it needs no explanation
for finding ways to define
the meaning of any reason
to enjoy a glass of wine.

Raise your glasses
make a toast
drink slowly
savor it.

Rejoice
in the contemplation
of self redemption
imposed
by circumstances
around
the soapbox
we are on.

INSATIABLE THOUGHTS

A whirlwind of ideas
staged in front of my voice
flashes across the horizon
appearing within the length
of my insatiable thoughts.

Nothing new coming across
no weaving a self reliance
while I seemingly feel lost.

And yet
I only let go of emotions
without making a concession
without a consideration
for any intent but my own.

That is the way I bring reason
to the words of my new song
hoping that someday
whoever
pays attention to this music
may forever
fall in love
with vibrations from my soul.

FULFILLED

Tender moments of admission
to close in.

A simple decision to be made
at ease...
        at will
with the understanding
of not having to regret
any mutual corresponding
move
sequestered by vivid eyes
willingly
inviting to dive into the
pleasure of smiling lips.

This was not a lusting thought
but a closure for a poem.
leaving me somehow fulfilled.

VECTOR

A pointless vector
of indifference
easily helped by the
luck of commitment
while at the same time
projecting...
sparkles of its own beliefs
will soon succumb to an angle
of zero degrees.

BIG WASTE

We all know that conflict is part of life
but good intentions will define
the venues to find solutions
trying to make everything just fine.

Yet
ignorance...
wants to be heard
although often can be blind
by surrounding circumstances
shouting words very sublime.

Most of us know that too often
it is a big waste of time.

RINGING BELL

By now much has been thought out
and said
even written
so today
any concern
about what's to be said
it is not much a concern
to be grasped as news.

I for one
I'm not a sesquipedalian
yet confronting a blank
piece of paper
I want nothing but being frank
by penning down ideas coming to mind.

The more the better. My thoughts may not be
important
to whom is aiming to judge
the meaning or lack of rhyme
I express in poetry.

I write just for exercise. Any athlete
knows the importance of sacrifice
a big effort being inflicted everyday
so the poet is no difference and he/she must know well
how to use the words awaiting the ringing of his/her bell.

COMMODITY

Time
is a commodity
not in the hands of the mortals.

Running free
and unopposed
it finds no way of being told
to get off
and mind its own business.

Time is only borrowed
and available to us
while it last.

On Earth
time can be wasted
or be counted on
yet... time
is no more than time
in the sense of its own meaning
- the occurrences in life.

GRATIFYING

As humbling as it can be,
the perils of revising anything
we have written once or twice...
maybe three times or more,
especially poetry,
it's for sure an obligation
we poets must go though
and endure
to succeed.

It is an odious task.

Yes indeed,
it takes time away from productivity.

I agree,
but it is also gratifying
by enhancing the belief,
that anything we write
deserves the most attention
by providing an honest effort,
before our own eyes;
including the ones of the readers...
along the powers that be.

BEING IN ECSTASY

One inch at the time
the lips are closing in
and the dual rhythm of breath
became just one
maintaining the pace
not wanting to let go.

The hugging
caressing
the one more long kiss
tender and lovely as she is
to me.

Oh yes the warmth of two bodies
rushing to giving in to pleasure
wrapped in each other's arms.

Such a relief
of being in ecstasy
one inch at the time
even if it were a dream.

FLOWING RIVER

Deep into the countryside
all around there is an inviting
opportunity
to find a lyrical scene
of impressionism at its best.

By taking a moment
easy breathing settles in
as a witness of such a wonder of nature.

Suddenly a sign of modern times
with opalescent ideas
is taking form to stay put
inviting to anyone to making sense out of it.

It is a surrealist occurrence
waiting to set up the pace
in front of a trembling ambiguity
of choices to be made.

An unexpected rain threatens
to keep falling down
while the flowing river
happily serpentines
between meadows
in extinction
due to eager
and impatient housing developers

who could not wait anymore
to build along the river bank.

\- - -

TANKA (Weather Forecast)

The sun is out there
winking its eyes to stay on.
The clouds are playful
while the wind is very strong.
Today's forecast call for rain

ELEVEN POEMS in Haiku

The decent humor
wanting to remain at such
must laugh at itself.

\- - -

While turning the wheels
the wagon is in motion
we can go places.

\- - -

The shadows of greed
reoccur within the time
confronting a will.

\- - -

The words not spoken
or shown on any paper
can't be heard or read.

\- - -

Pondering raindrops
the thought of moving ahead
makes me feel alive.

\- - -

Some choices in life
keep dancing in front of us
the music is loud.

\- - -

An outstanding gift
is the joy of having health
while keeping it up

\- - -

Such a full silence
and yet a ticking rhythm
keeps crawling in verse.

\- - -

The fear is present
the new abnormality
is taking its place.

\- - -

Applying pressure
to anything we have lost
makes no sense at all.

\- - -

Not telling the truth
deserves a heavy payment
along interest.

TWO WORDS

Veracity
and duality
are two simple rhyming words
keeping up with the velocity
imposed by signs on the roads
we travel daily.

One takes us to the truth
the other ends in two faces
that somehow can bring discord.

So let us be careful and use words
wisely...
to complete this last strophe.

IN A SHELL

Living in our own shell
may create the full illusion of
feeling totally safe.

And so most of us believe it
but carefully observing
from the inside
we may be sort of defenseless
we cannot see
clearly
nor can we hear the
noise taking place outside.

Forget about thinking...!

The walls we are surrounded by
are oblivious to our existence
or any attempt to dream
in a shell.

UNDERSTOOD

Plenty of poems well written
when carefully read...
they shall bring vibrations of joy
produce an envious experience
from which to learn
and yet
for the reader to be moved
the poem has to be brilliant
and completely understood.

TRAIN RIDE

In the train ride
of our life
it is not the speed we travel
nor the number of stations
we pass by….

It's the people that we meet
at the station to get on.

It's the company we keep
while we share conversation
inspiring us to move on.

But oh yeah… that final day
where we all have to get off
the train ride
of our life
we could tell from one another
who was lucky to be in love
with the person we have traveled
even if the trip was short.

LOGS OF WOOD

It is Friday night
we gather around in a circle
waiting for a chance to read
if possible poetry.

Others...
instead of verse they read prose.

Having an addiction to the spoken word
most of us know each other by now
yet there are always a few
who appear to be new
and interested
in the group.

With a timing anxiety we watch
logs of wood
being converted into ashes
but the fire keeps on burning
providing attractive flames...
the warmth is welcome
cherished by all
patiently waiting the turn
to speak and be heard
inhaling some of the smoke
in the air.

TO AGREE TO DISAGREE

Often
being around the fire
can warm up our desire
of being content... at ease.

Not only with ourselves
but in the company of others
their opinions making us converse
in harmony.

An exchange of ideas
in the pursuit to believe in
that the right way to achieve
something...
must be fully put in place
and acknowledged
while mutual attention is given
to one another.

Then we could simply make a point
to agree to disagree
and keep on breathing in peace.

Photo from Internet- Image pexels.com

REFLECTING FACTS

What appears to be down
it may actually be up there.

It is not something for real
but a reflection
on water clearly for us to admire.

Like a simple association
of nature
 features
   or people
     even thoughts
at our feet
gathered in plain sight
at the mercy of the mind.

ESCAPING

To the West of my ideas
lays a verse not understood
written with a good intention
soothing rhyme and comprehension
rooted in an Eastern attitude
that somehow is out of fashion
according to the best intentions
of the brains that be.

Yet I should not put aside
the foreign accent of my words
even though I keep on veering to the North
of simple thoughts
escaping out of the South of my mind...
unmercifully in spiral
and often with no control
of a direction in destiny.

About the author :

Emiliano Martín, author of **"Spain´s Footprints in Philadelphia"** came to the U.S., as an Immigrant in 1971. He established his residence in the city of Philadelphia. Presently he lives with his family in Bucks County, Pennsylvania.

With a passionate voice possessed by drama, he has presented his poetry in many schools, radio, TV and Cultural Centers. For years he has been involved in the poetry scene as a performing poet and organizer of events. In 1988 he founded "Northeast Philadelphia Poetry Forum" being its director for three consecutive years. Also former president of Círculo Español of Philadelphia, from 1989 till 1992 he served as Executive Director of "Latin American Guild for the Arts" (LAGA) in Philadelphia. In October of 2018 he became elected President of "Pennsylvania Poetry Society."

His poems have been published in many issues of Philadelphia Poets, Mad Poets Review, Schuylkill Valley Journal, Lit Fuse, US 1, Plume Magazine of F&M College, Stepping Stones, Big Intersection, BCCC- Robert Fraser annual reading collection of poems and other U.S. periodicals, as well as Spanish language publication in Spain, like Mizares, Marejadas and Bulletin of Club C.C.C. de Madrid.

With his new book of poetry **"Around the Fire"** there is another interesting look at the way the author views and observes some of the moments of life. His writings go on.

Other titles by the author :

Spain's Footprints in Philadelphia (2020)
Daydreaming in Verse (2019)
Vulnerable Excellence (2019)
511Aphorisms of my Humor (2010)
Dream and Shadows (2002)
Moody Muse (2001)
In the Company of Time (1999)
Whirlwind of Thoughts (1998)
Glazed by the Moon (1996)
In the Wilderness (1995)
Sparkles of Eternity (1994)
The Legacy of a Poet (1988)

(Also in the Spanish language)

Coplas Aforismos y Diretes (2020)
Huellas de España en Filadelfia (2020)
Fuimos de la COE (2019)
...Including some twenty plus unedited manuscripts

Emiliano Martín